THE BIGGEST UPSET OF THE DECADE

President Donald J. Trump
and The Theories Behind His Win

Duke F. Calhoun

MP Publishing

Copyright

© 2017 by Duke F. Calhoun

Table of Content

Introduction

Before Donald J. Trump became the 45th and current President of the United States, he was a business magnate, a television personality, and a highly controversial figure all rolled into one. Some of his unorthodox words and notorious remarks had built for him a reputation that he carried for much of the extent of his 2016 presidential campaign, making him a favorite target for the media. From promises such as the limitation of visas and green cards for immigrants to the construction of a "border wall" between Mexico and the United States, Trump's planned policies had garnered much criticism on the national and international landscape. Adding fuel to the fire were several scandals that plagued his reputation, such as a scandalous recorded conversation and allegations of sexual misconduct. Soon, many were quite convinced that, given the state of affairs surrounding Trump, his presidential bid will be a failure.

In spite of all this, the man undeniably shocked the world when he won the presidency.

The reactions across the country and the world were a combination of celebrations and outcries, while some were still reeling from the residual shock and disbelief at the results to even speak. Still, it was undeniable; despite losing the popular vote to Democratic presidential candidate Hillary Clinton at 46.09% to 48.18%, Trump had garnered the most electoral votes at 304 compared to Clinton's 227, ensuring a win in his bid for the presidency.

From journalists to political commentators to celebrities, from Rachel Maddow and Megyn Kelly to Miley Cyrus and Seth MacFarlane, many presented their sentiments regarding Trump's win, most of them made in fear and disgust at what is to come under a Trump presidency. Elsewhere in the country, actual protests and riots took place as many liberals and pro-Democrats took to the streets and demanded that the election results be reversed, all while Trump took to the stage and made his victory speech at a hotel in New York.

Naturally, from the time Trump had won to the present day, many have begun analyzing and considering the factors that had contributed to what the media had dubbed "a shocking upset" in the presidential elections. Many articles and thought pieces that were still gripped by the jolt of the elections' outcome all beg the question: How did Donald J. Trump, amidst all the controversy and against a highly qualified Democratic candidate in Hillary Clinton, win the presidency?

THE ROAD TO THE PRESIDENCY

There is much to be said about Trump's presidential campaign run, which officially began when he announced his bid to run for the presidency on June 26, 2015 at Trump Tower, presenting his campaign slogan Make America Great Again, often shortened to #MAGA. During his announcement, Trump had presented the issues and programs that would become the backbone of his campaign, ranging from illegal immigration, the country's national debt, and the threat of Islamic terrorism.

Due to Trump's "colorful" remarks and policies as well as his reputation, most analysts and media commentators dismissed his run as trivial and even facetious. Before and during the campaign, many of the aforementioned personalities expressed the opinion of the majority: that while Trump was undeniably an "interesting" personality at best, his chances at winning the presidency were next to none. News programs and media outfits were quick to deliver news of Trump's "outrageous" remarks, which seemed to come around frequently whenever he made public speeches during his campaigns in other states. For the most part, Trump ignored the naysayers during his campaign and instead stuck to his policies and programs. Throughout his campaign, there have been many controversial moments and statements covered by the news, though there are a choice few that stand out due to their notoriety or simply their overall impact on the voting public.

Trump versus Illegal Immigration

Making up a large portion of Trump's controversial policies were his immigration policies, which were covered extensively by the media and his speeches.

To start off, Trump called for a rollback on "birthright citizenship," which aimed to cancel the citizenship of children born in the U.S. to undocumented immigrant families, going against the Fourteenth Amendment's Citizenship Clause which generally agreed that those born on U.S. soil are automatically made American citizens regardless of their parents' citizenship. Another of

Trump's policies was the RAISE Act, which stood for Reforming American Immigration for a Strong Economy; the act sought to reduce legal immigration to America by 50% by reducing the numbers of issued green cards by half and thus putting a limit on annual refugee admissions at 50,000. Economic studies at Penn Wharton posited that, in spite of the act's aims, it would weaken the economy in the long run instead of strengthening it, as an estimated 4.6 million people would become unemployed and the economy would become 2% smaller by 2040.

Perhaps the most controversial of Trump's immigration policies, as mentioned before, were his plans for the Mexico-United States Barrier, a mass deportation plan for illegal immigrants, and a complete ban on Muslim immigrants. As early as during his declaration to run for the presidency, Trump had proposed a plan to build a border wall that would prevent illegal Mexican immigrants from crossing the border into the United States. Part of the controversy surrounding the plan is Trump's declaration that Mexico will pay for the wall to be built, partly for "allowing" their undesirables cross the border into the country. Trump, in return, stated that the wall only aimed to keep illegal immigrants out, and that the plan was merely to have a "big, beautiful door" stand between Mexico and the United States, through which legal immigrants can walk through freely and feel welcomed in the country.

Many criticized Trump's plan for the border wall, positing arguments about the funding that would go behind its construction (the estimated build cost is predicted to be around $25 billion, not including private land acquisitions and fence maintenance, and the annual maintaining cost to be at $750 million per year), as well as the long-term ineffectiveness that it would have at stopping the entry of illegal immigrants unless agents were present to patrol at all times; experts explained that illegal immigrants often entered the country by using duplicitous documents and overstaying visas as well as being smuggled into the country, making a border wall rather ineffectual.

Trump's proposed "mass deportation" plan, announced as early as August 2015, focused again on illegal immigrants who would "[get] out and [get] out fast" as soon as he becomes president. Though Trump expressed his sentiments with the term "mass deportation" as used by the media, he iterated that the plan must be followed, with priority of deportation given to illegal immigrants who have committed crimes and/or have overstaying visas. Like with the border wall plan, criticism flooded Trump's planned mass deportation policy, citing an economic and fiscal backlash should the proposal ever be put into effect.

Lastly, Trump's proposed full Muslim immigration ban focused initially on "banning all Muslims" from entering the country, though this has since been softened into "banning all immigrants from countries with a history of terrorism," or at least those tied with Islamic terror. An added measure was to have a database that would track Muslims in the States, as well as expanded surveillance in mosques across the country. This plan came in the wake of the deadly November 2015 Paris attacks, as well as the 2015 San Bernardino shooting. Criticism for the ban came in droves, explaining that the plan only strengthened stereotypes made against Muslim immigrants, whose Muslim heritage often linked them to Islamic terror in the eyes of certain people. Sadiq Khan, London's first Muslim mayor, decried Trump's narrow views over Islam as "dangerous" and "divisive."

Trump and Climate Change

Another one of Trump's widely debated policies is his stand on global warming and climate change. Trump counts himself as one of those who believe that global warming is merely a hoax invented by the Chinese to make U.S. manufacturing non-competitive. He added that China does not do anything to support climate change, being free to burn fossil fuels while undercutting the United States on manufacturing.

Trump admits that he is not that great of a believer of what he calls "man-made climate change," despite the presence of scientific data and evidence gathered and processed by quite literally all major scientific institutions in the United States that global warming is indeed a stark and potentially dangerous reality for the world. There is even evidence to back up the fact that most of climate change experienced today is man-made.

Trump's "non-believer" stance on climate change and global warming merely added more notoriety to his reputation amongst critics and detractors, especially after he made it clear that he wished to repeal the regulations made by former President Barack Obama's

Environmental Protection Agency, which saw the closure of several coal-fired power plants across the country in order to limit carbon emissions that contributed to global warming. To take things one step further, Trump also endorsed the withdrawal of the United States from the 2015 Paris Agreement.

The accord was presented by the United Nations Framework Convention on Climate Change (UNFCCC) and agreed upon by over 195 countries present during the United Nations Climate Change Conference of 2015, when Barack Obama was still the POTUS. The accord aimed to impose limitations and monitoring on the carbon emissions of participating countries, which would then hypothetically put a stop to the increase of global average temperature and keep it at "well below 2 °C above pre-industrial levels."

As with his arguments on climate change, Trump believed that the accord greatly limited America's industrial output considerably, thus allowing it to be overtaken by China (who ironically was one of the signees of the Paris Agreement). During his campaign and well into his first 100 days as president, Trump promised to revitalize coal industries which he believed were greatly set back by environmental limitations, and this revitalization included the shunning of the statutes of the Paris Agreement and an executive order which reversed environmental regulation programs, including ex-President Obama's Clean Power Plan.

Withdrawal from the Paris Agreement and from the UNFCCC will take a process of up to four years, meaning that by the time Trump achieves the goal of withdrawing the United States from the accord's regulations, the 2020 U.S. presidential elections will have already taken place a day prior. Thus, it still remains to be seen whether Trump will be in position long enough to see the withdrawal come into fruition, or if another president will take the reins and even make another choice.

Sexual Misconduct and the Access Hollywood Recording

In a possible effort to create a smear campaign against Trump and derail his momentum in the campaign, some scandals about him surfaced as late as a few weeks before the elections. The gist of these was that Trump was accused of sexual misconduct, wherein he was said to have kissed and groped up to 12 women without their consent. Compounding this also was a recorded 2005 conversation between Trump and television and radio host Billy Bush (who was also a member of the Bush family), wherein Trump was recorded bragging that he was able to kiss and grope women any time he wanted because of his celebrity status.

Though Trump himself had openly denied any allegations of sexual misconduct and apologized for what he called "locker room talk," many of his critics implied that what he had been doing amounted to sexual assault. Some, even those from the Republican Party, called for Trump's withdrawal from the presidential race and having his running mate Mike Pence take over as the Republican presidential candidate instead. Expectedly, anti-Trump voters and those supporting Hillary Clinton used the scandal to fuel public outcry against Trump, with Clinton echoing the sentiments of Trump's critics that Trump should never be allowed to become president.

However, if there were detractors joining the clamor against Trump, there were also those who saw the advantages of the scandal's leak, including former White House chief strategist Stephen Bannon. According to Bannon, the scandal became a "litmus paper test" that helped Trump pinpoint any Republican allies who were not supporting him fully, allowing him to refrain from granting such allies positions in his Cabinet. An example of such would be New Jersey Governor Chris Christie, who was denied a Cabinet position after publicly denouncing Trump on WFAN in the wake of the scandal.

Certain Republican members of Congress, after facing severe backlash from supporters after their public denouncement of Trump, conceded in the end that they will still support him in the elections. Some of these included Senator John Thune of South Dakota and Representative Scott Garrett of New Jersey, though at the time they did not refer to Trump by name and instead generically called him "the Republican ticket." Such turnaround support may have been instrumental in Trump's success in winning the electoral vote, despite the near-miss he had taken in losing support from some in his own party.

Along with his denials and apologies, Trump turned the scandals around and pointed instead towards Hillary Clinton and her husband, former President Bill Clinton. Trump reminded the public of Bill Clinton's scandal with Monica Lewinsky as well as his alleged sexual misconduct with three other women, and mentioned that Hillary Clinton was an "enabler" who bullied and discriminated her husband's alleged victims.

BEHIND THE WIN

On November 8, 2016, many were already sure that a Hillary Clinton presidency was in the bag. Live coverages were already voicing their opinions that the elections would be over with Trump simply not winning the presidency. As the official tallies were updated throughout the day, though, silence and disbelief set in as Trump gradually overtook Clinton and maintained a lead with the electoral votes, ending with Clinton calling Trump to concede the elections even as certain states were said to be still too close to call.

Journalists from news channels covering the elections, from CNN to MSNBC, were left stunned as Trump took to the podium and made his first public address as president-elect. Elsewhere, posts and messages on social media were tuning in to express outrage and incredulity at the results, and mass protests sparked up in no time at all in an effort to denounce Trump's election win. Since then, numerous people have wondered what exactly made

Trump win the presidency, given his track record during the campaign. These are but a few of the factors that may have contributed to the Trump victory.

Media Coverage

It was no secret that throughout the campaign, Trump was a candidate who enjoyed unprecedented media coverage whenever he made press conferences or campaign appearances. Even before Trump had officially declared that he was running for president, the media had already made him a highlight in their news, when his political remarks against terrorism and illegal immigration were starting to make waves in the news. This leads to the notion that perhaps Trump won because of the coverage he had received, which was propagated throughout social media in the form of articles, news videos, and thought pieces.

Naturally, there are arguments that explain that the media (that is, both social media and mainstream media in general) should not be blamed for Trump's ascendance into the presidency. As an article in The Atlantic posits, it is the voters who have helped Trump win, not the media coverage of his campaign, and that the media simply covers what it chooses to. As there has been no solid proof to indicate that a bona-fide way of helping an individual's platform take off is through continuous media exposure, the argument laid forth in the article seems more sensible than the assumption that the media should be blamed outright for Trump's upset victory.

However, while the media should not be blamed for ushering in a Trump presidency, it is also worth noting that the exposure Trump has gotten may still have an effect on the voters who watched the coverage of the campaign. Trump was notorious for disdaining political correctness, and was never afraid of making his statements blunt and sometimes brutal, adding to his controversial mystique which his supporters found solid and his detractors detestable. As such, Trump has been ingrained into the minds of the people through the media to the point that some could not help but become interested in what he has to say. After all, while the media may control what and who to cover on the news, it cannot control what the viewers (who are, in this case, also voters) would make of the coverage and how it would affect their mindset. The media cannot control what a viewer-voter would do after seeing Trump deliver a press conference address on live television, nor can they dictate what a viewer-voter would see once he/she researches online out of a desire to read "behind the lines" of Trump's blasé and often condemned statements.

The process then shifts: perhaps the viewer-voter managed to take a look at Trump's platform and surmised that he had a few well-meaning points behind his straightforwardness. Perhaps, given this notion, the viewer-voter would tune in to future news coverage of Trump and see something else that would further pique his/her interest in the candidate. This, in turn, could give a viewer-voter a change of heart about Trump's ideologies and policies, or strengthen further any support he/she has if he/she was a Trump supporter to begin with. Obviously, it would be erroneous to assume that this effect is the only result to be expected from the extensive media coverage of Trump's campaign, but it does have a hypothetical believability, and it may have been a key contributing factor behind Trump's victory with voters in certain states which, up until the elections, were believed to have been pro-Clinton or at least anti-Trump.

It also does not seem to help that, during Trump's first 100 days as president, the media coverage on him has been found to be 80% negative, according to a Harvard study. Of course, the media's less-than-favorable stance towards Trump stems from his own hatred of the media, where on several occasions he has called out certain news organizations for being biased and propagating "fake news," and has denied them the leeway of covering press briefings. Trump's supporters would see the media's treatment of him as an attack on his integrity, the same integrity he had displayed during the campaign which made him a favorable candidate in the eyes of many, if the results of the elections are taken as proof.

For example, certain Trump supporters cried foul over the media bias regarding the alleged Russian interference that saw Trump win the presidency, as well as the leaks of the allegations of sexual misconduct and the Access Hollywood recording; they say that while the media focuses on these issues in an effort to "destabilize" Trump's presidency, potential election fraud perpetrated by the Democrats is being denied or ignored outright. This, in turn, only further reinforced the support of Trump's most ardent followers, who assumed that the issues on Trump were nothing more than attacks made in an effort to stop him from running. These, in turn, allowed him to circumvent some of the backlash he had received; while his critics kept calling for his withdrawal, his supporters doubled down on their backing of him, possibly adding more to the momentum that was contributory in helping him win.

In effect, support for Trump may erode for as long as the media continues to cover his most controversial and most detestable words and deeds on the news, but the support may also be further strengthened as well, as Trump's supporters would use any bias that the media may have against him to decry the one-sided public coverage he may be getting. And again, there is the hypothesis that continuous media coverage of Trump can influence a viewer-voter into at least listening to what he has to say.

Vox Populi

Another factor that may have cemented Trump's victory was his vocal and blunt approach to the campaign and to the elections in general. Unlike most politicians before him, who preferred to stay within the boundaries of political correctness, Trump was unafraid and unabashed with his statements, whether in the so-called "Twittersphere" to the top of a stage on a podium. In a day and age where politically incorrect statements and individuals are often frowned upon, to say the least, Trump's candid and brutal honesty led many of his supporters to acknowledge him as someone who could say what he wished to, and was not afraid of any consequential liberal backlash.

In relation to the term "liberal," liberals refer to people who focus on the ideologies of equality and liberty. They often speak out against discrimination and maltreatment, whether the matter is related to race, religion, sexuality, or social status. While this ideally makes their stance honorable, some liberals are sometimes perceived in the political and cultural landscape as condescending, narrow-minded, and judgmental especially to those of a different opinion than theirs. It is common to see videos online of liberals participating in many rallies or protests, spewing obscenities towards the focus of their outrage and sometimes even verbally and physically accosting any individuals present who have a different stance to take. In fact, it is also relatively common for altercations to take place in such situations wherein some liberal groups participate in destruction of property, obstruction of traffic, and harassment of civilians, adding more flak to their reputation. This, of course, does not apply to all liberals; it merely echoes the prevalent idea among the people that liberals are of a single-minded opinion, and that they tend to attack anyone who would counter that opinion.

With this growing unpopular opinion towards liberals and their ideologies borne from recorded videos and articles documenting them, some tend to harbor indignation and resentment towards liberals. However, they cannot publicly take on them, sometimes for fear of backlash and retribution, sometimes simply because liberals have the numbers advantage. However, with Trump's rise in the presidential campaign, many of these silent protesters seem to have found in him a speaking voice which encourages them to express their sentiments the same way he does, especially since he presented himself as someone who listens to the plight of the masses. In some way, if Trump supporters would be considered "the masses," then Trump has turned himself into "the voice of the masses," vox populi. Trump's "infectious" brashness and openness during his public addresses further fueled his supporters' fervor during his campaign rallies in certain states, to the point where any anti-Trump protesters in the crowd would be quickly booed out of the venue and even downright assaulted. On one occasion, Trump said that he will pay for any legal fees if his supporters end up being charged for beating up any hecklers or protesters disrupting the rallies.

While this notion does not excuse the blatant racism, stereotyping, and animosity displayed by both sides on numerous occasions during the campaign, it does lend credence to the idea as to why Trump had won the presidency. In him, many of his supporters felt that they could finally go out and voice their indignations and grievances to what they feel is a society that has forgotten and forsaken its creed. In the same way many liberals flock together in order to speak their principles and ideologies, many of Trump's voters managed to band together to make a national wave that saw Trump take the elections with the biggest upset of the decade, something that the media and most anti-Trump personalities severely underestimated. With Trump as their shining paragon, Trump supporters who were formerly confined to a passive stance before now take to the streets and to social media actively in order to make themselves heard. By banding together under the banner of Make America Great Again, they helped Donald Trump become the 45th POTUS.

Tuning Out, Staying Strong

Some of the reasons as to why support for Trump soared during his presidential run in spite of his many controversies may be of a psychological factor. An article at Vox presented the argument that perhaps "motivated ignorance" is what plays a large factor among Trump supporters. When interviewed about the scandals and issues faced by Trump and his administration at present, certain Trump supporters mention that they would simply "tune out" the news reports of the scandals and avoid digesting it outright. In relation to motivated ignorance, such "tuning out" was characteristic in people regarding politics, wherein it is mentioned the people simply prefer to ignore the truth in favor of their principles and views rather than acknowledge something that makes them uncomfortable. Additionally, in banding together under a shared reality with other people of the same mindset as they have, individuals choose to avoid hearing anything from the opposing side for fear of cognitive dissonance. Simply put, people remember and appreciate information that caters to their worldviews more than information that undermines or counters them.

This is possibly what keeps support for Trump high; instead of acknowledging and processing the negative information related to Trump in the scandals and issues he faces, his supporters choose to listen to what they feel fits their opinions and perspectives.

There is also the idea that support for Trump remains relatively unchanged not because certain supporters love Trump, but rather because they loved their families and country enough to be "fearful of what was [going to] happen if Hillary Clinton got elected president." As Trump's campaign revolved around #MAGA and a concern for the country's welfare, Trump supporters dedicated their support to Trump's rhetoric and that "they wouldn't leave Trump for anything." Such love for the country is a common motif among the staunchest of Trump's supporters, and they present this unwaveringly as they denounce media organizations that have "devoted" themselves full-time to the president's destruction out of what is perceived as a revenge lust for the defeat of Hillary Clinton.

The Blue-Collar Appeal

Trump enjoyed an appeal in blue-collar and working-class precincts, such as in Pittsburgh and Pennsylvania, mainly due to his stand against multilateral free trade agreements and his promise of reintroducing industries that have been severely limited or shut down altogether due to environmental regulations. For example, in Greene County in southwestern Pennsylvania (one of the states where Trump won by a "razor-thin margin"), Trump reigned undisputed among voters due to the region's blue-collar nature and the fact that coal-mining was the county's economic lifeblood. With mines being shut down, many miners and workers lose their jobs and soon struggle to make ends meet.

Compared to Trump, Clinton faced backlash in 2016 from other coal-mining states such as West Virginia due to her comments on putting mines "out of business" in a bid to look for cleaner renewable energy sources. While she does add that she does not wish to forget the workers and miners who would undoubtedly lose their jobs in the process, her statements already had their negative effect on blue-collar voters. With Trump's promise of reopening mines and revitalizing the coal-mining industry, on the other hand, many former miners who had gone bankrupt from a dying industry see this as a chance to return to a line of work that pays more than present opportunities, at as much as $150,000 annually compared to $30,000 annually. Between choosing a candidate who would close down or limit their livelihood to a candidate who promises to return that livelihood to them, voters in areas like Greene County have no questions about who to choose.

Such states started out as "solidly Democratic," when labor unions were much stronger and work opportunities were thriving under mills and mines, but gradually swerved as circumstances dwindled. Those whose livelihoods in their states depended on coal and steel stated that Trump was akin to "a breath of fresh air [that] has created jobs." Others have simpler beliefs; with frustration stemming towards the status quo, some think that while Trump's promises coming true can be unlikely, they are at least content with the idea that he will try his best to fulfill them.

Going against the negatives of free trade, as mentioned above, is also appealing to voters who have an eye for Trump. According to him, free trade is what steals jobs from most hardworking Americans. In his view, as with a majority of working-class Americans, the current policies on free trade mean that factories and industries pack up and move elsewhere, leading to hardworking laborers losing their jobs in the process. While those in a "higher" spectrum, such as economists, officials, learned individuals and media personalities laud free trade as wholly good and economically boosting as it ideally means being competitive and progressive in the global sense, those in the "lower" spectrum see it as a danger to their livelihoods, much like the environmental and economic regulations that lead to mines and mills closing down and causing laborers to lose their jobs.

As the businessman that he undoubtedly is, Trump managed to win the eyes and ears of the working class Americans who potentially suffer grievances from the effects of free trade. In his speeches, Trump won over a large chunk of the working class by explaining that free trade is what leads "corrupt elites" to convince manufacturers and industries to move out into other countries such as Mexico for global "competitiveness" and manufacturing when they could have stayed and effectively prevented their workers from losing their jobs. Trump also claimed that the government (with extra blame on Obama and Clinton for promoting free trade) does nothing to alleviate this, as they simply run into every agreement or negotiation with countries, never minding that they would end up getting the short end of their deals, all because it is ensured that they would get "massive campaign contributions" from those facilitating the deals.

Of course, like with most of Trump's claims, no sufficient evidence is present to back up some of his claims (which most of his critics point out), but his words rang loud and clear nonetheless in the ears of hardworking Americans who had suffered because of its effects. For the most part, Trump is not wholly against free trade, but he does have a protectionist stance on the concept, believing that imposing tariffs and quotas on other countries to protect local manufacturers and businesses. He has made plans on changing the regulations behind NAFTA (the North American Free Trade Agreement) and the TPP (Trans-Pacific Partnership), and vows to stop China from "stealing" jobs and money from the country.

In the span of one year since his election into office, Trump has had varying stands on free trade, although he does keep reiterating that he will make good on his promises of stopping companies from moving abroad to manufacture goods, and rehashing trade agreements for the country's benefit. While Trump's many critics and rivals are quick to point out the long-term difficulties and consequences that Trump's protectionist stance on free trade will have, to a blue-collar American who has lost a job from companies moving abroad due to such trade deals, Trump's promises may be worth hearing and even supporting.

The Bernie Sanders "What-If"

For a long time after the most unanticipated election results of the decade came out and confirmed that Trump had won the presidency, many debated on whether Bernie

Sanders would have won if he, not Hillary Clinton, had been the one to face Trump in the elections.

The 76-year old junior U.S. Senator from Vermont started out with the bid to gain the Democratic Party's nomination as their ticket, with Clinton being his chief competitor. While he mostly ran as an independent, Sanders aligned himself mostly with the Democrats, with whom he shared similar political ideals and viewpoints. During his campaign, most of Sanders' political platforms included promoting awareness for climate change (a stark contrast to Trump), economic inequality, and public funding for college students. Moreover, unlike most major presidential candidates, Sanders declined using super PACs (political action committees) to fund his campaign, instead opting to take direct individual campaign donations from supporters. Adding to his campaign, as most of Sanders' supporters were also internet and social media savvies, he had a strong campaign run launched and backed in social media sites such as Twitter, Tumblr and Facebook, crowned by the hashtag #FeelTheBern.

In terms of polls, Sanders did relatively well, leading with 4% ahead of Clinton in New Hampshire during the Democratic primaries, while trailing her by only 3% in Iowa. A poll conducted in Quinnipiac University showed Sanders leading ahead of Clinton by 5%, adding proof to his popularity among young voters. He would also go on to defeat Clinton by large margins in the primaries in Washington, Hawaii, Alaska, and his home state of Vermont, while also pulling off an upset victory in the Michigan primary, where polls initially favored Clinton. In an NBC/Wall Street Journal poll hypothesizing a Trump-Sanders presidential race, Sanders gained 53% votes to surpass Trump's 39%.

With a strong following and a populist appeal, Sanders seemed primed to become the Democrat ticket. To the great disappointment of his supporters, however, Sanders was sidetracked in favor of Clinton as the Democrat candidate, and he stepped down as a candidate and opted to simply support Clinton in a bid to fight a Trump presidency. Many began to imagine what factors led to his failure to gain the party's nomination.

For one thing, Sanders lacked the advantages of a super PAC that Clinton had. While it was deemed honorable on his part to take a grassroots approach, his campaign rallies demanded large funds that simply could not be attained by taking individual donations. Additionally, he failed to find backing in states that could make up for his loss of momentum from ceding other states to Clinton, while Clinton managed to gain some backing from states that mostly support Sanders, further weakening his push.

Secondly, Sanders had setbacks among non-whites, trailing behind Clinton amongst blacks and Hispanics in the primaries. Some speculate that perhaps Sanders was simply relatively unknown amongst them that he failed to convince them to support him, while some suggest that Clinton's supporters simply had solid reasons to stick by her as the Democrat ticket. Additionally, Sanders lacked support from most conservative pro-Democrats, who feel that his liberal-leaning views did not cater to ideals they were familiar with.

Another hypothetical speculation was that the public viewpoint towards liberals affected the idea of voting for a strong candidate in Sanders. As mentioned above, the radical perspectives of most young liberals (who made up the bulk of Sander's voters) and the antagonism or resentment they show to those who disagree with them may have contributed to a loss in appeal towards Sanders from other voters. In part, such radical or liberal thinking is also said to have influenced some liberals to vote for Clinton, who was reared to hopefully become the first female POTUS. Because such liberal thinking usually does not sit well with conservatives, it may have had an impact on Sanders' chances of being chosen as the Democrat candidate.

Lastly, the crux of Sanders' defeat came from his lack of support from the Democratic Party itself, as Clinton was already the party's solid choice for the presidential race. Adding insult to injury was a series of DNC (Democratic National Committee) emails released by WikiLeaks. In the emails, a plan to undermine Sanders' campaign in favor of Clinton was revealed, with DNC officials even planning to introduce Sanders' religion as a campaign issue to further destabilize his run. DNC chair Debbie Wasserman Schultz also spoke unfavorably of Sanders in the emails, stating that Sanders did not understand the Democratic Party. Famed historian and political activist

Noam Chomsky remarked that, had it not been for the pressure put on him by Obama-Clinton backers in the party, Sanders would have won the Democratic Party's nomination.

Therefore, again the question is asked: would Sanders have defeated Trump if they were the final candidates to head into the race? With only hindsight to help, only hypothetical answers have been made to address such a question. However, given that Sanders undoubtedly had the backing of the majority of liberals and young voters, and that his planned policies had an anti-elitist appeal that would have sat well with other voters, many would agree that Bernie Sanders likely would have been a more difficult candidate for Trump to overcome.

Benghazi and the Email Controversy

While the sexual misconduct allegations and the Access Hollywood recording both marred Trump's presidential run, it is quite possible that the so-called "email controversy" and the House Committee hearings on Benghazi weighed more in dictating the votes in certain states.

The background of the controversies was that during Clinton's tenure as the Secretary of State, between 2009 and 2013, she had been using a private email server at her home instead of using the official State Department accounts and server. Upon investigating, the State Department found that almost 2100 of the emails processed in Clinton's private server were determined to be classified. Because Clinton had potentially violated State Department protocols and security procedures for handling such information on a private server, the controversy garnered criticism towards Clinton, with various experts and officials remarking that Clinton had violated federal laws in maintaining a private server and handling classified information there.

Clinton's supporters decried the controversy's timing as well as then-FBI Director James Comey's interference, which all took place a mere two weeks before the election and in the wake of the allegations on Trump, stating that the nature of the email controversy's leak aimed to damage Clinton's integrity as a presidential candidate while shifting the focus away from Trump's scandals. Most explained that in spite of the clandestine nature of maintaining a private email server instead of using a secure State Department server, there was really no bearing to the idea that Clinton had mishandled the information she was processing. Indeed, the FBI soon acquiesced that while Clinton's actions were seen as careless, there were no grounds for her to be charged legally for what happened. Additionally, certain news articles offered that the criticism for Clinton to use a secured government server instead of her own private server was flawed as certain government servers, including that of the State Department's, were non-secure as well; the State Department's server, in fact, was brought low by a cyberattack that was labeled the worst ever inflicted on a U.S. federal agency.

Still, while the email controversy did have points that made it seem like a political attack against Clinton more than an actual scandal, it was the Benghazi hearings that may have provided the final nails in the coffin for Clinton's presidential run.

Beginning on May 2014, the House Committee aimed to shed light on the September 11, 2012 Libyan attacks that took the lives of U.S. Ambassador to Libya J. Christopher Stevens, Foreign Service officer Sean Smith, and CIA contractors Glen Doherty and Tyrone Woods. As Secretary of State at the time, Clinton had a responsibility to reveal to the public the nature of the attacks, but instead opted alongside the Obama administration to disseminate a different narrative: that the attacks were caused by the actions of an angry mob.

Such a cover-up was said to have come after the State Department failed to act upon the danger faced by the department's outpost and a nearby CIA annex in the purlieu of Benghazi. Despite warnings by a State Department officer who was dispatched there nine months prior to assess the threat, officials of the Obama administration failed to take any precautionary measures to ensure that the officials in the outpost and annex would be safe. More flak came as people started questioning other points of the controversy, such as the risk of having outposts in a place as dangerous as Benghazi, and the absence of any rescue attempts or defenses in spite of military assets in the area.

Moreover, in a supposed relation to the email controversy, Republican officials in the House Committee hearing on the Benghazi attacks asserted that Clinton had deleted the emails on her private server on October 2014, including emails between her and confidant Sidney Blumenthal regarding the Benghazi attacks. Clinton maintained that the emails she had deleted were of a personal nature, and that she had handed over all other emails to the State Department for investigation. Clinton's campaign staff and Democrat allies rebuked the accusations, stating that the Republicans were merely "clinging on their invented scandal" in the effort to further damage Clinton's reputation.

The issue and the subsequent cover-up did not sit well with the public, especially as the false reports of a mob attack were maintained for at least a few days by Clinton and even then-President Barack Obama before officials decided to reveal the truth at last. Many saw the handling of the incident as a lack of competence and a betrayal of public trust on the part of the administration and Clinton. It also did not help that the attack came not long after then-President Obama's declaration that the threat of the Al-Qaeda and its affiliates ended with Osama Bin Laden's death, serving as a wake-up call that the threat of terrorism was still at large even after Operation Neptune's Spear had been a success.

And so, as seen side by side, it appears that Clinton's controversies far outweighed that of Trump's. While the scandals and allegations that Trump faces are no less repulsive, perhaps the public saw that the legal and security nature of Clinton's issues far outweighed something that appealed more on the moral and politically correct sense, especially when it meant having either person become the next POTUS. Clinton undoubtedly had the experience and background needed to become president over Trump's business savvy, but perhaps the email controversy and the issue on Benghazi made the voting public realize that in spite of such qualifications, she could make far worse mistakes in the future when no chances must be taken. These lapses in judgment and the failure to act accordingly beforehand may have caused a major shift in public opinion for her and the Democrats. Indeed, many feared that Clinton's presidential aspirations may have been damaged beyond repair, and her 2016 loss to Trump may be a testament to that.

ONE YEAR AFTER

Even after Trump had been inaugurated into the White House and taken his place as the newly elected President of the United States, the figurative fires have not gone out yet. News coverage is highly focused on documenting almost his every move, dogging every policy or program in the works while offering insight and criticism on those already implemented.

In his first 100 days as president, Trump had already renewed public scrutiny towards his immigration policies after he had implemented Executive Order 13769, or the infamous "Muslim ban," the regulations of which included the suspension of the U.S. Refugee Admissions Program for 120 days, the reduction of the number of refugees to be admitted into the country, the indefinite suspension of the admission of Syrian refugees, and the 90-day suspension of entry of refugees whose country failed to meet the adjunction standards of the U.S. immigration law. Almost as soon as the order was executed, national and international denunciation of it spread broadly, and various courts convened to issue temporary restraining orders to ban most of its major provisions. In response, Trump drafted Executive Order 13780 as a replacement, which limited travel to the U.S. from various countries and refugees who did not possess a visa or valid documents. Trump called the second order "a watered down, politically correct version" of the previous one.

Trump also signed Executive Order 13767, or the Border Security and Immigration Enforcement Improvements, which sought to fulfill his promise of a crackdown on the entry of illegal immigrants from Mexico by building the notorious border wall he had promised. The bill called for the illegal detainment and deportation of illegal immigrants as well as an order for the U.S. Customs and Border Protection to hire up to 5,000 additional border patrol agents. While prototypes for the wall are said to be under construction already, the U.S. Congress has not yet allotted any funds into the wall's actual construction, and thus the plan for the border wall has not yet begun.

With regards to his stand on free trade, Trump made good on his promise of reviewing all trade agreements that the

U.S. currently has, and that if a deal would harm the United States economy or its laborers, then it will be renegotiated. Though Trump also promised to take down the NAFTA with Canada and Mexico, he has since opted to renegotiate the deal instead of canceling it altogether.

On his 100th day into the presidency, Trump signed the Executive Order on the Establishment of Office of Trade and Manufacturing Policy, which aimed to stimulate U.S. manufacturing, decrease trade deficit, and create more work. The office was assigned to handle the renegotiation of U.S. trade deals and reclaim U.S. factory jobs in accordance with Trump's promises during the campaign. Experts, however, were quick to point out that it was automation and not trade deals that caused workers to be dropped by their companies, and that the policies that Trump and his officials aim for could create a trade war.

While the North American Free Trade Agreement may live to see another day, Trump fulfilled his intention of taking down the Trans-Pacific Partnership. On January 2017, he issued a presidential memorandum calling for the withdrawal of the United States from the TPP, and called instead for a focus on pursuing negotiations that would promote American industry, raise wages, and protect workers.

Trump also bunkered down on his promises to rescind environmental regulations as well as those from Obama's Clean Power Plan in an effort to reinvigorate the coal industry. While it is assumed that employment in coal plants will be unlikely to come back in great numbers Trump nonetheless kept his word in directing federal agencies to annul any environmental regulations that hamper the development of energy resources. Republican congressmen saw the action as a promotion of energy independence, while critics of the administration denounced it as contributory to worsening climate change.

Currently, apart from his outrageous remarks and tirades against what he calls a biased media, Trump has not gotten past his sexual misconduct allegations just yet. One of Trump's chief accusers who may play a key in a possible impeachment is ex-Apprentice contestant Summer Zervos, who claimed that Trump had kissed and groped her without her consent at a Beverly Hills hotel back in 2007. When Trump publicly denied the claims and called Zervos out for lying in his campaign, Zervos sued Trump for defamation. With Gloria Allred as one of her lawyers, Zervos also called for a subpoena on Trump and his campaign team, calling on them to release any documents they possess that involve the allegations of Trump's sexual misconduct. In response, Trump's lawyers called for a dismissal of the case, which is still going on currently. Anti-Trump personalities are hopeful that these allegations will lead to his impeachment from office.

This came after the Supreme Court acceded that a president cannot be sued only if the charges laid against him are related to his official duties; an example of this would be ex-President Bill Clinton, who was sued for alleged sexual harassment when he was still governor of Arkansas, a charge which ended with Clinton's impeachment by the House of Representatives.

To be sure, Trump is making waves in a way similar to Barack Obama after the latter became the first African-American President of the United States, and no doubt the press will continue to hound Trump up until 2020, when he will try to get reelected into office. Would his campaign by then be similar to his campaign back in 2016? Will he learn from the mistakes of his previous run and take the measures necessary to strengthen his future campaign? What more scandals or issues will arise to try and derail Trump's hopes for a continued presidency?

Perhaps this would be the time that anti-Trump voters can rally and stop another four years of a possible Trump presidency. Conversely, perhaps Trump's supporters by then have seen many of their grievances addressed and their pleas answered, renewing the same resolve they had when they proudly shouted Make America Great Again back in 2016. Many things would have already taken place by 2020, and no doubt many experts would offer suppositious opinions or predictions as to what exactly will happen in the four years of Trump's presidency.

Only time will tell what is in store for Trump. However, he can at least brag about one more thing: that he overcame the odds stacked against him in 2016 and, by a big swerve in circumstances, became the 45th President of the United States.

ABOUT THE AUTHOR

Duke F. Calhoun is the pseudonym used by a Philippine-based freelance writer. Calhoun has been writing content for articles on certain websites on the Internet for almost two years now under various editors. In his free time, he focuses mostly on gaming and on researching material that he uses in his creative works, including his work-in-progress Dogs of War: Soldiers of Fortune.